365 American Eng
by Michael DiGiac......, ...

Paperback Edition

Published in New York, USA
January 2014

To Gloria...thanks for editing

ISBN: 978-0-9915079-0-0

A Message From Michael

Thank you for purchasing 365 American English Idioms. My name is Michael DiGiacomo, and I am a native New Yorker. I have been helping language students learn English since the early 1990's. I began my formal language-teaching career in Sendai, Japan in 1994. Since then, I have worked in the ESL field as an instructor, a teacher trainer, an academic director, and a language school director. In 2004, I earned an MBA in Global Management. Now, I am the owner of Happy English, an English tutoring company in New York City. I teach students from all over the world here in New York, and online in their country.

I believe that language study should be both enjoyable and practical. In 2010 I started a website to provide a variety of English lessons to students all over the world. I set out to create lessons that were practical, easy to understand, and useful for self-study. Many of my students have given me ideas and suggestions for lessons and this book grew out of some of those ideas.

You can find my website at **www.myhappyenglish.com**

Idioms are commonly used in everyday, conversational English. Using idioms in your conversation will make your English more colorful and interesting. I encourage you to study the lessons in this book, and begin using these idioms in your conversations today! You will sound more natural when you do so.

Please note that this book use American English idioms and American English spelling.

As always, thanks for studying with me.

Table of Contents

Key Points About Idioms

An idiom is a group of words that go together as a set phrase. It is usually not possible to guess the meaning of the phrase because the meaning of the phrase itself is generally quite different from the meaning of the words used in the phrase.

For example, let's look at the idiom **a pain in the neck**. Looking at the words literally, the phrase **a pain in the neck** seems to mean a kind of medical problem. Let's see this idiom in use:

Renewing my driver's license was **a pain in the neck**. I had to take time from work, because the office is not open on the weekend. Then, I needed to wait for almost three hours there!

Can you guess the meaning of **a pain in the neck** from this example? It is not a medical problem... **A pain in the neck** means "bothersome" or "inconvenient."

In this book, I am going to teach you 365 idioms. That's an idiom a day. I suggest you study and memorize one idiom every day. The best way to memorize the idioms here, or to memorize any vocabulary, is use that idiom in a sentence that is true in your life. So for example, if renewing a driver's license is **a pain in the neck** where you live, just memorize the sentence I wrote above. Otherwise, try to think of another situation (or person) that is "bothersome" or "inconvenient" for you and create your own sentence.

Good luck, and thanks for studying with me!

1: a cup of joe

How to use it:

- You can buy, drink, make, etc. a cup of joe.

Explanation:

- Joe is a slang word for coffee and so a cup of joe means a cup of coffee.

Example:

- I like to start my day with a cup of joe.

2: a dime a dozen

How to use it:

- [something] is a dime a dozen

Explanation:

- A dozen means twelve, and a dime is a ten-cent coin, so a dime a dozen literally means twelve costs ten cents. So if something costs a dime a dozen, it is inexpensive or easy to find.

Example:

- Hot dog carts are a dime a dozen on the streets of NYC.

3: a pain in the neck

How to use it:

- [something] or [someone] is a pain in the neck

Explanation:

- Something that is a pain in the neck is troublesome and inconvenient.

Example:

- Tom is a pain in the neck. He borrows my tools but never returns them on time.

4: a piece of cake

How to use it:

- [something] is a piece of cake

Explanation:

- Something that is a piece of cake is easy to do.

Example:

- Using computers is a piece of cake for me.

5: a pipe dream

How to use it:

- [something] is a pipe dream

Explanation:

- A pipe dream is something unrealistic that you wish for or wish to do.

Example:

- I know sailing a yacht in the South Pacific is a pipe dream, but someday I hope to do it!

6: a screw up

How to use it:

- [someone] is a screw up

Explanation:

- A screw up is a person who often makes careless mistakes, generally because they are not paying attention to what they are doing or because they are incompetent.

Example:

- I hear Tom was fired because he is a screw up.

7: absent-minded

How to use it:

- [someone] is absent-minded

Explanation:

- Someone who is absent-minded easily forgets things.

Example:

- Jack forgot his wife's birthday. He's so absent-minded.

8: add fuel to the fire

How to use it:

- [something] or [someone] adds fuel to the fire

Explanation:

- Someone who adds fuel to the fire makes a bad situaion much worse.

Example:

- Bob added fuel to the fire by yelling at his boss.

9: all heart

How to use it:

- [someone] is all heart

Explanation:

- Someone who is all heart is a very kind person.

Example:

- Ted is all heart, so everyone likes him.

10: all over the map

How to use it:

- [something] or [someone] is all over the map

Explanation:

- Something or someone that is all over the map is very disorganized.

Example:

- The CEO's speech was all over the map.

11: all set

- [something] or [someone] is all set

Explanation:

- Something or someone that is all set is ready.

Example:

- We've prepared well, so I think we are all set for the meeting.

12: all thumbs

How to use it:

- [someone] is all thumbs

Explanation:

- Someone who is all thumbs is very clumsy.

Example:

- Ted said he is all thumbs when it comes to repairing something.

13: an arm and a leg

How to use it:

- [something] costs (or) [someone] pays an arm and a leg

Explanation:

- Something that costs an arm and a leg is very expensive.

Example:

- It costs an arm and a leg to buy beer at a baseball stadium.

14: as quiet as a mouse

How to use it:

- [something] or [someone] is as quiet as a mouse

Explanation:

- Something or someone who is as quiet as a mouse is very quiet.

Example:

- Jen's new boyfriend was as quite as a mouse.

15: as sick as a dog

How to use it:

- [someone] is as sick as a dog

Explanation:

- Someone who is as sick as a dog is very sick.

Example:

- Bob was as sick as a dog because he caught the flu.

16: at the drop of a hat

How to use it:

- [someone] does something at the drop of a hat

Explanation:

- When you do something at the drop of a hat, you do it immediately, without hesitation.

Example:

- I'd marry her at the drop of a hat.

17: back to square one

How to use it:

- [something] or [someone] is back to square one

Explanation:

- When you go back to square one, you start again from the beginning.

Example:

- My boss rejected my work, now it's back to square one.

18: bark is worse than one's bite

How to use it:

- [someone]'s bark is worse than their bite

Explanation:

- Someone whose bark is worse than their bite is not actually as mean or angry as they appear to be.

Example:

- The new boss seems strict, but his bark is worse than his bite.

19: bed head

How to use it:

- [someone] has bed head

Explanation:

- Someone who has bed head has strange looking hair because of the position their head contacted the pillow when they were sleeping.

Example:

- I woke up with bed head this morning.

20: bed of roses

How to use it:

- [something] is a bed of roses

Explanation:

- Something that is a bed of roses is very comfortable.

Example:

- Traveling for business seems glamorous, but is it no bed of roses.

21: bend over backwards

How to use it:

- [someone] bends over backwards

Explanation:

- When you bend over backwards you do more than what is expected of you.

Example:

- Bob always bends over backwards to help someone.

22: bent out of shape

How to use it:

- [someone] is bent out of shape

Explanation:

- When someone is bent out of shape, they are angry and upset.

Example:

- Jack was bent out of shape because his flight was cancelled.

23: big enough to swing a cat

How to use it:

■ [somewhere] is big enough to swing a cat

Explanation:

■ When a place is big enough to swing a cat, it is spacious.

Example:

■ It's a bright apartment, but not big enough to swing a cat.

24: bite one's tongue

How to use it:

■ [someone] bites their tongue

Explanation:

■ When you bite your tongue, you stop yourself from saying something that might make another person angry or upset.

Example:

■ Even though Jim was angry, he bit his tongue.

25: bite the bullet

How to use it:

- [someone] bites the bullet

Explanation:

- When you bite the bullet, you deal with an unpleasant situation.

Example:

- Jim has had a toothache for a month. He has to bite the bullet and go to the dentist.

26: blow a fuse

How to use it:

- [someone] blows a fuse

Explanation:

- When you blow a fuse, you become very angry.

Example:

- Tom blew a fuse when the truck hit his new car.

27: blow one's top

How to use it:

- [someone] blows their top

Explanation:

- When you blow your top, you become angry.

Example:

- Jane blew her top when she saw her boyfriend in a café with another girl.

28: break someone's heart

How to use it:

- [someone] breaks another person's heart

Explanation:

- When you break someone's heart, you disappoint them romantically.

Example:

- Ted broke Mary's heart when he left her.

29: break the bank

- [something] breaks the bank

Explanation:

- When you break the bank you spend a lot of money.

Example:

- Pam broke the bank at the mall yesterday.

30: break the news

How to use it:

- [someone] breaks the news to another person

Explanation:

- When you break the news to someone, you tell them bad news.

Example:

- We had to break the news to Jake that his pet fish died.

31: break up with

How to use it:

- [someone] breaks up with another person

Explanation:

- When you break up with someone, you end a romantic relationship with them.

Example:

- Ken broke up with Marie last night.

32: breeze through

How to use it:

- [someone] breezes through something

Explanation:

- When you breeze through something, you have an easy time doing it.

Example:

- Tom breezed through his TOEFL exam.

33: bring home the bacon

How to use it:

- [someone] brings home the bacon

Explanation:

- When you bring home the bacon, you support your family.

Example:

- Jack brings home the bacon.

34: button one's lip

How to use it:

- [someone] buttons their lip

Explanation:

- When you button your lip you stop speaking.

Example:

- The teacher told little Joey to button his lip.

35: call the shots

How to use it:

- [someone] calls the shots

Explanation:

- Someone who calls the shots is the authority.

Example:

- Tom is the boss, but the office manager calls the shots.

36: calm someone down

How to use it:

- [someone] calms another person down

Explanation:

- When you calm someone down, you help them become relaxed.

Example:

- Classical music really calms me down.

37: cat got [someone's] tongue

How to use it:

- the cat got [someone's] tongue

Explanation:

- When the cat got your tongue, you are unable to speak.

Example:

- Jim was pretty quite at the party, so I asked him if the cat had gotten his tongue.

38: catch some rays

How to use it:

- [someone] catches some rays

Explanation:

- When you catch some rays, you are getting a suntan.

Example:

- It was sunny so I caught some rays today.

39: catch Z's

How to use it:

- [someone] catches Z's

Explanation:

- When you catch Z's you sleep.

Example:

- I'm going to catch some Z's before dinner.

40: caught red handed

How to use it:

- [someone] is caught red handed

Explanation:

- When you are caught red handed, you are caught while doing something wrong.

Example:

- Bob was caught red-handed sleeping in the office.

41: change of heart

How to use it:

- [someone] has a change of heart

Explanation:

- When you have a change of heart, you change your decision about something.

Example:

- The boss was going to give us a day off tomorrow, but it looks like he's had a change of heart.

42: chase rainbows

How to use it:

- [someone] chases rainbows

Explanation:

- When you chase rainbows, you are trying to do something impossible.

Example:

- Tom has been trying to date Lisa for several months now, but she always refuses him. I think he is chasing rainbows.

43: chew the fat

How to use it:

- [someone] chews the fat with another person

Explanation:

- When you chew the fat, you have a leisurely chat.

Example:

- I was chewing the fat with Tommy last night at the bar.

44: chicken out

How to use it:

- [someone] chickens out

Explanation:

- When you chicken out, you loose your courage.

Example:

- I was going to go sky diving, but I chickened out.

45: cold turkey

How to use it:

- [someone] goes cold turkey

Explanation:

- When you quit or go cold turkey, you stop doing something abruptly.

Example:

- Jim stopped smoking cold turkey.

46: collect dust

How to use it:

- [something] collects dust

Explanation:

- When something collects dust, it is not being used.

Example:

- My old stereo set is just collecting dust.

47: come a long way

How to use it:

- [something] or [someone] comes a long way

Explanation:

- When something has come a long way, it has improved greatly.

Example:

- Mayumi's English has come a long way since last year.

48: come clean

How to use it:

- [someone] comes clean

Explanation:

- When you come clean, you admit wrongdoing.

Example:

- Ted came clean about taking the money from the company.

49: come down with a cold

How to use it:

- [someone] comes down with a cold

Explanation:

- When you come down with a cold, you are ill.

Example:

- Tom came down with a cold from the air conditioner at work.

50: come in handy

How to use it:

- [something] comes in handy

Explanation:

- When something comes in handy, it is useful and makes life more convenient.

Example:

- A second car in the family would come in handy.

51: come like clockwork

How to use it:

- [something] or [someone] comes like clockwork

Explanation:

- When something comes like clockwork, it comes precisely on time.

Example:

- The trains in Tokyo come like clockwork.

52: crack open a cold one

How to use it:

- [someone] cracks open a cold one

Explanation:

- When you crack open a cold one, you open a cold beer.

Example:

- At the end of the work day Paul likes to crack open a cold one.

53: crack someone up

How to use it:

- [something] or [someone] cracks another person someone up

Explanation:

- When you crack someone up, you make them laugh.

Example:

- Comedians like Steve Martin really crack me up.

54: dead from the neck up

How to use it:

- [someone] is dead from the neck up

Explanation:

- When someone is dead from the neck up, they are not very intelligent.

Example:

- The new salesman is nice, but dead from the neck up.

55: dead in the water

How to use it:

- [something] is dead in the water

Explanation:

- When something is dead in the water, it can not progress or move ahead.

Example:

- Because of the red tape in the office, our proposal is dead in the water.

56: dead quiet

How to use it:

- [something] is dead quiet

Explanation:

- When someone or something is dead quiet, it is very quiet.

Example:

- In the suburbs, it is usually dead quiet at night.

57: dead-end job

How to use it:

- [someone] has a dead-end job

Explanation:

- When you have a dead-end job it is a job with no possibility for promotion or advancement.

Example:

- Tom said he quit because it was a dead-end job.

58: dirt cheap

How to use it:

- [something] is dirt cheap

Explanation:

- When something is dirt cheap, it is very cheap.

Example:

- I bought some suits in Bangkok for dirt cheap.

59: dish the dirt

How to use it:

- [someone] dishs the dirt with another person

Explanation:

- When you dish the dirt, you gossip.

Example:

- Jill and Carol spent the afternoon dishing the dirt about their neighbors.

60: do away with

How to use it:

- [someone] or [an organization] does away with [something]

Explanation:

- When you do away with something, you abolish it.

Example:

- The café did away with the free refill policy.

61: the dog days of summer

How to use it:

- [we say this about hot summer weather] These are the dog days of summer

Explanation:

- The dog days of summer are the hottest days in the summer.

Example:

- I'm getting tired of the dog days of summer.

62: dog eat dog world

How to use it:

- [we say this about life] It is a dog eat dog world

Explanation:

- A dog eat dog world is a very competitive situation.

Example:

- It's a dog eat dog world on Wall Street.

63: dog tired

How to use it:

- [someone] is dog tired

Explanation:

- When you are dog tired, you are very tired.

Example:

- I worked until 10 last night and I'm dog tired.

64: done to a turn

How to use it:

- [some food] is done to a turn

Explanation:

- When something is done to a turn, it is cooked perfectly.

Example:

- The chicken was done to a turn.

65: down to earth

How to use it:

- [someone] is down to earth

Explanation:

- Someone who is down to earth is practical and not pretentious.

Example:

- Lori's new boyfriend is down to earth.

66: down to the wire

How to use it:

- [something] is down to the wire

Explanation:

- When a situation is down to the wire, the deadline is very near.

Example:

- It was down to the wire, but I finished my report.

67: drag one's feet

How to use it:

- [someone] drags their feet

Explanation:

- When you drag your feet, you intentionally do something slowly.

Example:

- I told Jack to stop dragging his feet and finish his work.

68: draw a blank

How to use it:

- [someone] draws a blank

Explanation:

- When you draw a blank, you can't remember something.

Example:

- I was trying to remember his name but I drew a blank .

69: dressed to kill

How to use it:

- [someone] is dressed to kill

Explanation:

- When you are dressed to kill, you are wearing sexy clothes.

Example:

- Jenny was dressed to kill last night at the club.

70: drink like a fish

How to use it:

- [someone] drinks like a fish

Explanation:

- When you drink like a fish, you drink a large amount of alcoholic drinks.

Example:

- Cathy's a nice person, but she drinks like a fish.

71: drive someone up a wall

How to use it:

- [something] or [a person] drives someone up a wall

Explanation:

- Someone or something that drives you up a wall annoys you greatly.

Example:

- His laziness in the office drives me up a wall.

72: ducks in a row

How to use it:

- [someone] has their ducks in a row

Explanation:

- Someone who has their ducks in a row is organized.

Example:

- The new salesman got all his ducks in a row in just a week.

73: everything but the kitchen sink

How to use it:

- [something] has everything but the kitchen sink

Explanation:

- Something that has everything but the kitchen sink has many options.

Example:

- My pizza has everything but the kitchen sink on it.

74: face the music

How to use it:

- [someone] faces the music

Explanation:

- When you face the music you take responsibility for wrongdoing.

Example:

- Jim broke his mom's vase, so he'll have to face the music when she gets home from work.

75: fender bender

How to use it:

- [someone] has a fender bender (with their car)

Explanation:

- When you have a fender bender, you have a minor auto accident.

Example:

- Jack had a fender bender with the company car.

76: fight an uphill battle

How to use it:

- [someone] fights an uphill battle

Explanation:

- When you fight an uphill battle you are struggling with something.

Example:

- I want to ask my boss for a few days off, but I think I'll be fighting an uphill battle.

77: fish or cut bait

How to use it:

- [someone] has to fish or cut bait

Explanation:

- When you fish or cut bait, you make a decision.

Example:

- Jim took too much time thinking about his problem, so I told him it was time to fish or cut bait.

78: fish out of water

How to use it:

- [someone] feels like a fish out of water

Explanation:

- Someone who feels like a fish out of water is in an unfamiliar and uncomfortable situation.

Example:

- Since I don't know the rules, I felt like a fish out of water at the stadium.

79: fit as a fiddle

How to use it:

- [someone] is fit as a fiddle

Explanation:

- Someone who is fit as a fiddle is in good health.

Example:

- Grandpa had a medical examination and he is fit as a fiddle.

80: fit for a king

How to use it:

- [something] is fit for a king

Explanation:

- Something that is fit for a king has superior quality.

Example:

- The suite at the hotel was fit for a king.

81: fit to be tied

How to use it:

- [someone] is fit to be tied

Explanation:

- Someone who is fit to be tied is very angry.

Example:

- Jane was fit to be tied when her husband came home at 11pm.

82: flash in the pan

How to use it:

- [someone] is a flash in the pan

Explanation:

- A singer or actor who is a flash in the pan is very popular for just a short time.

Example:

- A lot of pop singers are just a flash in the pan.

83: fly by the seat of one's pants

How to use it:

■ [someone] flies by the seat of their pants

Explanation:

■ When you fly by the seat of your pants, you do something without prior training.

Example:

■ When I tried to repair my computer, I was flying by the seat of my pants.

84: foot the bill

How to use it:

■ [someone] foots the bill

Explanation:

■ When you foot the bill, you pay the bill.

Example:

■ Jack foot the bill when he took us to the restaurant.

85: from the bottom of one's heart

How to use it:

- [someone] does something from the bottom of their heart

Explanation:

- When you do something from the bottom of your heart, you do it very sincerely.

Example:

- I appreciated her help from the bottom of my heart.

86: from the get-go

How to use it:

- [someone] likes someone from the get-go

Explanation:

- When you like something or someone from the get-go, you do it from the beginning.

Example:

- Jean is really nice. I liked her from the get-go.

87: full of hot air

How to use it:

- [someone] is full of hot air

Explanation:

- Someone who is full of hot air speaks insincerely.

Example:

- I think that salesman was full of hot air. He said the car was in good condition.

88: get a second wind

How to use it:

- [someone] gets a second wind

Explanation:

- When you get a second wind, you get new energy and feel refreshed.

Example:

- I got a second wind after taking a nap and a shower.

89: get along with

How to use it:

- [someone] gets along with another person

Explanation:

- When you get along with someone, you have a good relationship with them.

Example:

- Kathy gets along with Ted's parents.

90: get back to someone

How to use it:

- [someone] gets back to another person

Explanation:

- When you get back to someone, you reply to them at a later time.

Example:

- Let me check and I'll get back to you tomorrow.

91: get down to the nitty-gritty

How to use it:

- [someone] gets down to the nitty-gritty

Explanation:

- When you get down to the nitty-gritty, you deal with the fundamental or essential aspects.

Example:

- Hopefully, during this meeting we can get down to the nitty-gritty.

92: get down to the nuts and bolts

How to use it:

- [someone] gets down to the nuts and bolts

Explanation:

- When you get down to the nuts and bolts, you discuss the most important aspects.

Example:

- During the meeting we got down to the nuts and bolts right away.

93: get hitched

How to use it:

- [someone] gets hitched or [two people] get hitched

Explanation:

- When you get hitched, you get married.

Example:

- Ed and Chris got hitched in Las Vegas.

94: get off on the wrong foot

How to use it:

- [two people] get off on the wrong foot

Explanation:

- When you get off on the wrong foot, your relationship with the other person doesn't begin smoothly.

Example:

- I think we got off on the wrong foot when we met at the party.

95: get on one's nerves

How to use it:

- [someone] gets on another person's nerves

Explanation:

- When someone or something gets on another's nerves, it bothers them.

Example:

- The noise in this neighborhood gets on my nerves.

96: get one's feet wet

How to use it:

- [someone] gets their feet wet

Explanation:

- When you get your feet wet, you have your first experience doing something.

Example:

- I got my feet wet as a teacher in 1989.

97: get out of hand

How to use it:

- [something] gets out of hand

Explanation:

- When something gets out of hand, there is chaos.

Example:

- Everyone was arguing at the meeting so it got out of hand.

98: get pulled over

How to use it:

- [someone] gets pulled over by the police

Explanation:

- When you get pulled over, the police stop your car.

Example:

- Yesterday, Joe got pulled over for speeding on the highway.

99: get something

How to use it:

- [someone] gets something

Explanation:

- When you get something, you understand it.

Example:

- Don't ask me about algebra. I don't get it.

100: get something for peanuts

How to use it:

- [someone] gets [something] for peanuts

Explanation:

- When you get something for peanuts, you buy it for a low price.

Example:

- I got this new computer for peanuts!

101: get the boot

How to use it:

- [someone] gets the boot

Explanation:

- When you get the boot, you get fired from your job or asked to move out of home.

Example:

- Joe got the boot after he argued with the boss.

102: get the pink slip

How to use it:

- [someone] gets the pink slip

Explanation:

- When you get the pink slip, you get fired from your job.

Example:

- Because he made too many mistakes, the accountant got the pink slip.

103: get with it

How to use it:

- [someone] gets with it

Explanation:

- When someone tells you to get with it, they want you to hurry.

Example:

- She told me to get with it, but I was going as fast as I could!

104: gift of gab

How to use it:

- [someone] has the gift of gab

Explanation:

- Someone who has the gift of gab talks a lot.

Example:

- My sister has the gift of gab.

105: give someone a hand

How to use it:

- [someone] gives another person a hand

Explanation:

- When you give someone a hand, you help them.

Example:

- I asked Jack to give me a hand painting the house.

106: goes around in circles

How to use it:

- [someone] or [something] goes around in circles

Explanation:

- When a conversation goes around in circles it does not progress. When a person goes around in circles, s/he doesn't get to their point.

Example:

- At the meeting, Jim was going around in circles so the boss told him to get to the point.

107: go belly up

- [a business] goes belly up

- When a business goes belly up, it goes bankrupt.

- The new café in town went belly up after just six months.

108: go bonkers

- [someone] or [an animal] goes bonkers

- When someone goes bonkers, they get very excited.

- My dog goes bonkers for chicken.

109: go down the tubes

How to use it:

- [something] goes down the tubes

Explanation:

- When something goes down the tubes, it fails.

Example:

- Because of the weather, our plans for a party at the beach went down the tubes.

110: go for broke

How to use it:

- [someone] goes for broke

Explanation:

- When you go for broke, you risk everything to achieve something.

Example:

- Tom went for broke to open the café, and now the shop is a big success!

111: go out of one's way

How to use it:

- [someone] goes out of their way

Explanation:

- When you go out of your way, you do something extra for another person's benefit.

Example:

- The waiter went out of his way to make sure we enjoyed the meal.

112: go south

How to use it:

- [something] goes south

Explanation:

- When something goes south, it fails.

Example:

- Cathy's first date with Tim suddenly went south when his real girlfriend walked into the café.

113: go through the roof

How to use it:

■ [someone] goes through the roof

Explanation:

■ When the price of something goes through the roof, it becomes very high.

Example:

■ The price of gasoline went through the roof after the hurricane.

114: go to the dogs

How to use it:

■ [something] goes to the dogs

Explanation:

■ When something goes to the dogs, it is in disrepair.

Example:

■ The old house down the street has really gone to the dogs.

115: go-to guy

How to use it:

- [someone] is a go-to guy

Explanation:

- Someone who is the go-to guy is the key person or expert.

Example:

- In my office, Yalcin is the go-to guy for computers and high tech.

116: goof off

How to use it:

- [someone] goofs off

Explanation:

- Someone who goofs off wastes time and doesn't accomplish what they are supposed to do.

Example:

- Bob got fired for goofing off instead of working.

117: goof up

How to use it:

- [someone] goofs up

Explanation:

- When you goof up, you make a mistake.

Example:

- Jim goofed up a lot this week and the boss was angry.

118: graveyard shift

How to use it:

- [someone] works the graveyard shift

Explanation:

- When you work the graveyard shift, you work the overnight shift

Example:

- Jack is working the graveyard shift tonight at the hospital.

119: grease monkey

How to use it:

- [someone] is a grease monkey

Explanation:

- A grease monkey is an auto mechanic.

Example:

- I took my car to the local grease monkey and he did a great job of fixing it.

120: greased lightning

How to use it:

- [something] moves like greased lightning

Explanation:

- A car that is like greased lightning is very fast.

Example:

- His new car is like greased lightning.

121: green around the gills

How to use it:

- [someone] is green around the gills

Explanation:

- Someone who is green around the gills is ill.

Example:

- Joe looked a little green around the gills so the boss sent him home.

122: green thumb

How to use it:

- [someone] has a green thumb

Explanation:

- Someone who has a green thumb is good at gardening.

Example:

- My mom has a green thumb and grows a lot of flowers and vegetables.

123: guinea pig

How to use it:

- [someone] is a guinea pig

Explanation:

- Someone who is a guinea pig is the subject of an experiment.

Example:

- Lori cooked pasta for the first time and asked me to be the guinea pig.

124: half-baked

How to use it:

- [something] is half-baked

Explanation:

- A half-baked idea is a foolish idea.

Example:

- The boss didn't approve of Tom's half-baked idea to lower prices.

125: hang it up

How to use it:

- [someone] hangs it up

Explanation:

- When you hang it up at the office, you quit your job.

Example:

- When Jack turned 59, he decided to hang it up and retire.

126: hard sell

How to use it:

- [something] is a hard sell

Explanation:

- When someone gives you the hard sell, they put pressure on you to buy something.

Example:

- The car salesman tried to give me the hard sell, but I refused.

127: have a ball

- [someone] has a ball

- When you have a ball, you enjoy something.

- We had a ball at the amusement park yesterday.

128: have a crush on

- [someone] has a crush on another person

- When you have a crush on someone, you have new romantic feelings for them.

- I have a crush on Fay, but she loves another guy.

129: have a ghost of a chance

How to use it:

■ [someone] has a ghost of a chance

Explanation:

■ When you have a ghost of a chance, there is a low possibility for something.

Example:

■ Because of the company budget, the proposal has only a ghost of a chance of getting approved.

130: have a memory like a sieve

How to use it:

■ [someone] has a memory like a sieve

Explanation:

■ When you have a memory like a sieve, you cannot remember things well.

Example:

■ I was trying to remember Jack's phone number, but I have a memory like a sieve.

131: have a screw loose

How to use it:

- [someone] has a screw loose

Explanation:

- Someone who has a screw loose is a little bit strange.

Example:

- I think the new salesman has a screw loose.

132: have a thing for

How to use it:

- [someone] has a thing for another person

Explanation:

- When you have a thing for someone, you have romantic feelings for them.

Example:

- I think Lou has a thing for Pam. He is always trying to chat with her.

133: have an iron stomach

How to use it:

- [someone] has an iron stomach

Explanation:

- Someone who has an iron stomach has a strong stomach and can eat almost anything without feeling sick.

Example:

- Jack ate pizza, a donut and fried rice. He has an iron stomach.

134: have no spine

How to use it:

- [someone] has no spine

Explanation:

- Someone who has no spine has no courage.

Example:

- Ted can't confront his boss about the problem because he has no spine.

135: have the time of one's life

How to use it:

- [someone] has the time of their life

Explanation:

- When you have the time of your life, you have a very good time.

Example:

- I had the time of my life during my vacation.

136: have the upper hand

How to use it:

- [someone] has the upper hand

Explanation:

- Someone who has the upper hand has an advantage in a situation.

Example:

- The workers have the upper hand over management.

137: have time to kill

How to use it:

- [someone] has time to kill

Explanation:

- When you have time to kill, you have free time.

Example:

- I have some time to kill, so I'm heading to the mall.

138: have two left feet

How to use it:

- [someone] has two left feet

Explanation:

- Someone who has two left feet is not a good dancer.

Example:

- I don't go to dance clubs because I have two left feet.

139: head over heels

How to use it:

- [someone] is head over heels for [another person]

Explanation:

- When you are head over heels for someone, you have strong romantic feelings for them.

Example:

- Mike is head over heels for Jane. They're a cute couple.

140: heart of gold

How to use it:

- [someone] has a heart of gold

Explanation:

- Someone who has a heart of gold is kind and caring.

Example:

- David is a good guy and always willing to help someone. He has a heart of gold.

141: high and dry

How to use it:

- [someone] is left high and dry

Explanation:

- When someone leaves you high and dry, they abandoned you without helping you.

Example:

- The IT department left me high and dry when they took a week vacation.

142: hit a nerve

How to use it:

- [something] hits a nerve

Explanation:

- Something that hits a nerve makes you upset or angry.

Example:

- Her harsh comments really hit a nerve with me.

143: hit it off

How to use it:

- [two people] hit it off

Explanation:

- When two people hit it off, the get along well from the first time they met.

Example:

- Barb hit it off with Jeff and they're still such great friends.

144: hit or bust

How to use it:

- [something] is a hit or bust

Explanation:

- A movie can be either a success (a hit) or a failure (a bust)

Example:

- Is Johnny Depp's new movie a hit or bust?

145: hit the books

How to use it:

- [someone] hits the books

Explanation:

- When you hit the books, you begin studying.

Example:

- Bob's dad told him to turn off the TV and hit the books.

146: hit the ceiling

How to use it:

- [someone] hits the ceiling

Explanation:

- When someone hits the ceiling, they become angry.

Example:

- Fred hit the ceiling when he saw his girlfriend dancing with another guy.

147: hit the ground running

How to use it:

- [someone] hits the ground running

Explanation:

- When you hit the ground running, you begin something with a lot of enthusiasm.

Example:

- When the marketing department got the OK to begin the campaign, they hit the ground running.

148: hit the mark

How to use it:

- [someone] hits the mark

Explanation:

- When you hit the mark, your explanation is perfect.

Example:

- Jack hit the mark during the meeting when he explained the reasons for the decline in sales.

149: hit the sack

How to use it:

- [someone] hits the sack

Explanation:

- When you hit the sack, you go to bed.

Example:

- It's time to hit the sack. See you in the morning.

150: home stretch

How to use it:

- [someone] or something is in the home stretch

Explanation:

- When you are in the home stretch, you are in the final phase of something.

Example:

- We are in the home stretch of the semester. It's time to study for final exams.

151: hook, line and sinker

How to use it:

- [someone] believes something hook, line and sinker

Explanation:

- When you believe something hook, line and sinker, you believe it without any doubt.

Example:

- The boss believed Jim's excuse for being late hook, line and sinker.

152: hop, skip and a jump

How to use it:

- [a place] is a hop, skip and a jump

Explanation:

- A place, like a store or park that is a hop, skip and a jump away is very close.

Example:

- The pizza shop is a hop, skip and a jump from my office, so I have lunch there often.

153: hopping mad

How to use it:

- [someone] is hopping mad

Explanation:

- Someone who is hopping mad is very angry.

Example:

- Ted was hopping mad when his wallet was stolen.

154: hot under the collar

How to use it:

- [someone] is hot under the collar

Explanation:

- Someone who is hot under the collar is very angry.

Example:

- The boss was hot under the collar when Bob came to work late this morning.

155: in a jam

How to use it:

- [someone] is in a jam

Explanation:

- When you are in a jam, you are in a difficult situation.

Example:

- I was in a jam when my laptop broke, but one of my friends fixed it for me.

156: in a New York minute

How to use it:

- [someone] does [something] in a New York minute

Explanation:

- When you can do something in a New York minute, you can do it very quickly.

Example:

- Tom can cook a great meal in a New York minute.

157: in in full swing

- [an activity (party, meeting) or business) is in full swing

Explanation:

- Something that is in full swing is at the peak of it's activity.

Example:

- The new café's operations are in full swing and it is filled with customers.

158: in good shape

How to use it:

- [someone] is in good shape

Explanation:

- Someone who is in good shape is physically fit.

Example:

- My friend Ed goes to the gym every day, so he's in good shape.

159: in hot water

How to use it:

- [someone] is in hot water

Explanation:

- Someone who is in hot water is in trouble.

Example:

- Bill was in hot water with the teacher when he didn't hand in his report.

160: in my book

How to use it:

- [something] is [adjective] in my book

Explanation:

- Something that is [adjective] in my book is [adjective] in my opinion.

Example:

- In my book, pizza is the best food on earth!

161: in over one's head

How to use it:

- [someone] is in over their head

Explanation:

- Someone who is in over their head is in a difficult situation.

Example:

- Bob was in over his head when he became the head chef at a busy restaurant.

162: in stitches

How to use it:

- [someone] is in stitches

Explanation:

- When you are in stitches, you are laughing uncontrollably.

Example:

- I was in stitches watching my favorite comedian.

163: in the bag

- [a deal or negotiation] is in the bag

- Something that is in the bag is certain.

- It looks like John has his new work contract in the bag!

164: in the boondocks

- [a place] is in the boondocks

- Someone who lives in the boondocks lives in the countryside.

- My cousin Jane lives in the boondocks, but I live in the city.

165: in the long run

How to use it:

- [someone] does [something] in the long run

Explanation:

- When you accomplish something in the long run, you accomplish it eventually.

Example:

- Getting a master's degree is hard work, but in the long run it is worthwhile doing.

166: in the middle of nowhere

How to use it:

- [a place] in the middle of nowhere

Explanation:

- Something that is in the middle of nowhere is in a very remote area.

Example:

- The hotel I booked was in the middle of nowhere so it was nice and quiet.

167: in the pipeline

How to use it:

- [a future plan] is in the pipeline

Explanation:

- Something that is in the pipeline is forthcoming.

Example:

- Jack said his plans for a trip to Asia are in the pipeline.

168: jump through hoops

How to use it:

- [someone] jumps through hoops

Explanation:

- When you jump through hoops to accomplish something, you make a great effort and sacrifice to do it.

Example:

- Joe said he needed to jump through hoops in order to get the boss to approve his vacation.

169: just around the corner

How to use it:

- [an event] is just around the corner

Explanation:

- Something that is just around the corner is happening very soon.

Example:

- Nick and Lori's wedding is just around the corner. I need to buy a suit to wear to the ceremony.

170: kick back

How to use it:

- [someone] kicks back

Explanation:

- When you kick back, you relax.

Example:

- After dinner, Ted likes to kick back and watch TV.

171: kill time

How to use it:

- [someone] kills time

Explanation:

- When you kill time you spend idle time.

Example:

- I was killing time at the mall this afternoon.

172: know something like the back of one's hand

How to use it:

- [someone] knows something like the back of their hand

Explanation:

- When you know something like the back of your hand, you know it very well.

Example:

- I know NYC like the back of my hand because I was born and raised here.

173: know the ropes

How to use it:

- [someone] knows the ropes

Explanation:

- When you know the ropes you are very experienced.

Example:

- The new guy in sales really knows the ropes, so the boss likes him.

174: know zip

How to use it:

- [someone] knows zip

Explanation:

- When you know zip about something, you know nothing about it.

Example:

- I know zip about American football, even though I'm American.

175: labor of love

How to use it:

- [someone's work or job] is a labor of love

Explanation:

- Something that is a labor of love is done for interest and/or pleasure.

Example:

- I work a lot of hours at my job, but it is a labor of love.

176: leave someone in the dark

How to use it:

- [someone] leaves another person in the dark

Explanation:

- When you leave someone in the dark, you withhold information from them.

Example:

- Tom said his wife left him in the dark about her plans to have the house painted.

177: let the cat out of the bag

How to use it:

- [someone] lets the cat out of the bag

Explanation:

- When you let the cat out of the bag, you reveal a secret.

Example:

- Jack let the cat out of the bag when he accidentally mentioned Bob's retirement plans to the boss.

178: like there is no tomorrow

How to use it:

- [someone] does something like there is no tomorrow

Explanation:

- When you do something like there is no tomorrow, you do it quickly and energetically.

Example:

- Jack ate that pizza like there is no tomorrow.

179: like two peas in a pod

How to use it:

- [two people] are like two peas in a pod

Explanation:

- When two people are like two peas in a pod they are very similar.

Example:

- Chris and his brother are like two peas in a pod. They both like sports and fast cars

180: lock horns

How to use it:

- [two people] lock horns

Explanation:

- When you lock horns with someone you argue intensely.

Example:

- Tom and his wife locked horns about the household budget again.

181: look on the bright side

How to use it:

- [someone] looks on the bright side

Explanation:

- Someone who looks on the bright side views something optimistically.

Example:

- Cathy always looks on the bright side of things.

182: lose one's temper

How to use it:

- [someone] loses their temper

Explanation:

- When you lose your temper you get angry.

Example:

- Frank lost his temper when the kids broke his window with a ball.

183: lose the plot

How to use it:

- [someone] loses the plot

Explanation:

- When you lose the plot you become irrational and don't focus on your original intention.

Example:

- The company had problems because the CEO lost the plot.

184: love at first sight

How to use it:

- [someone] experiences love at first sight

Explanation:

- When you experience love at first sight, you fall in love the moment you meet someone.

Example:

- It was love at first sight for Ann and Allen.

185: love handles

How to use it:

- [someone] has love handles

Explanation:

- Someone who has love handles has excess fat around their waist.

Example:

- I need to exercise more and get rid of these love handles.

186: luck out

How to use it:

- [someone] lucks out

Explanation:

- When you luck out you become lucky.

Example:

- I lucked out and found a great parking spot.

187: lucky break

How to use it:

- [someone] gets or has a lucky break

Explanation:

- When you get a lucky break you get an opportunity.

Example:

- My sister got a lucky break and got a promotion at her job.

188: made for each other

How to use it:

- [two people] are made for each other

Explanation:

- Two people who are made for each other are perfectly compatible.

Example:

- Lori and Nick were made for each other.

189: make a big stink

How to use it:

- [someone] makes a big stink

Explanation:

- Someone who makes a big stink about something complains loudly.

Example:

- The man made a big stink to the waiter about a hair in his soup.

190: make a killing

How to use it:

- [someone] makes a killing

Explanation:

- When you make a killing doing something, you make a lot of money.

Example:

- Ted made a killing selling toys on the internet.

191: make a mint

How to use it:

- [someone] makes a mint

Explanation:

- When you make a mint doing something, you make a lot of money.

Example:

- Cathy made a mint selling her house in NYC.

192: make a pit stop

How to use it:

- [someone] makes a pit stop

Explanation:

- When you make a pit stop you stop by somewhere briefly.

Example:

- I usually make a pit stop at a cafe on the way to work.

193: make eyes at someone

How to use it:

- [someone] makes eyes at another person

Explanation:

- When you make eyes at someone you look at them romantically.

Example:

- That guy has been making eyes at me ever since I arrived at the party.

194: make good time

How to use it:

- [someone] makes good time

Explanation:

- When you make good time, you arrive quickly.

Example:

- We made good time because the highway was not crowded.

195: make one's blood boil

How to use it:

- [a situation] makes [a person's] blood boil

Explanation:

- Something that makes your blood boil makes you very angry.

Example:

- Seeing people leaving garbage on the beach makes my blood boil.

196: make one's hair stand on end

How to use it:

- [a situation] makes [a person's] hair stand on end

Explanation:

- Something that makes your hair stand on end scares you.

Example:

- Stephen King novels make my hair stand on end.

197: make one's skin crawl

How to use it:

- [a situation] makes [a person's] skin crawl

Explanation:

- Something that makes your skin crawl revolts you.

Example:

- Lori said spiders make her skin crawl.

198: make out like a bandit

How to use it:

- [someone] makes out like a bandit

Explanation:

- When you make out like a bandit you are financially successful.

Example:

- Fred is making out like a bandit with his new business.

199: make a racket

How to use it:

- [a situation] or [someone] makes a racket

Explanation:

- Someone who makes a racket is very noisy.

Example:

- The kids are making a racket outside. I wish they would be quite

200: make waves

How to use it:

- [someone] makes waves

Explanation:

- Someone who makes waves causes a lot of problems.

Example:

- Even though he didn't agree with the boss, Ted didn't speak up during the meeting because he didn't want to make waves.

201: man's best friend

How to use it:

- [a dog] is man's best friend

Explanation:

- Man's best friend is a nickname for a pet dog.

Example:

- Jason is a lover of man's best friend.

202: meat and potatoes

How to use it:

- [something] is the meat and potatoes of a situation

Explanation:

- The meat and potatoes of something is the main and important part of it.

Example:

- It took half an hour for the CEO to get to the meat and potatoes of his speech.

203: mickey mouse job

How to use it:

- [someone] does a mickey mouse job

Explanation:

- A mickey mouse job is a trivial and non-essential task.

Example:

- Cathy said she is tired of her boss giving her micky mouse jobs all the time.

204: mind one's business

How to use it:

- [someone] minds their business

Explanation:

- When you mind your own business you do not get involved in other people's matters.

Example:

- Jack told you to mind your business because he wants to solve his problem by himself.

205: mint condition

How to use it:

- [something] is in mint condition

Explanation:

- Something that is in mint condition is in very good condition.

Example:

- I bought an old APPLE IIe in mint condition at the flea market.

206: money to burn

How to use it:

- [someone] has money to burn

Explanation:

- Someone who has money to burn has a lot of extra money.

Example:

- Tom always goes to Vegas because he has money to burn.

207: next to nothing

- [something] costs (or) [someone] pays next to nothing for[something]

Explanation:

- When you pay next to nothing for something, you have paid a very cheap price.

Example:

- Tommy paid next to nothing for his bike.

208: night owl

How to use it:

- [someone] is a night owl

Explanation:

- Someone who is a night owl likes to stay up very late at night and sleep during the day.

Example:

- Kathy is a night owl, so she is usually on Skype until 3am.

209: not all there

How to use it:

- [someone] is not all there

Explanation:

- Someone who is not all there is a little stupid.

Example:

- The new guy in marketing is not all there, so the boss is worried about him.

210: not my cup of tea

How to use it:

- [something] is not [a person's] cup of tea

Explanation:

- Something that is not your cup of tea is something you do not like.

Example:

- Playing sports is really not my cup of tea. I prefer listening to music.

211: not playing with a full deck

How to use it:

- [someone] is not playing with a full deck

Explanation:

- Someone who is not playing with a full deck is a bit strange.

Example:

- That man looks like he's not playing with a full deck, so please stay away from him.

212: now and then

How to use it:

- [something] happens (or) [someone] does something now and then

Explanation:

- When you do something now and then, you do it occasionally.

Example:

- Now and then I like to have some sweet desserts.

213: null and void

How to use it:

- [a contract or an agreement] is null and void

Explanation:

- When a contract or agreement is null and void, it is invalid.

Example:

- If you try to repair your computer or cell phone by yourself, the warrantee will be null and void.

214: number cruncher

How to use it:

- [someone] is a number cruncher

Explanation:

- Someone who is a number cruncher has a job related to accounting.

Example:

- We submitted the budget to the number crunchers and now we are waiting for their response.

215: off the beaten track

How to use it:

- [a place is] off the beaten track

Explanation:

- When someone lives off the beaten track, they live in a very rural area.

Example:

- Jack has a nice house, but it is off the beaten track. I wish he lived closer.

216: off the mark

How to use it:

- [something] is off the mark

Explanation:

- Someone's comments that are off the mark are inaccurate.

Example:

- The mayor's comments on the subway problem were off the mark, and the citizens were upset.

217: off the top of one's head

How to use it:

- [someone] knows [something] off the top of their head

Explanation:

- When you do something off the top of your head, you do it without prior preparation.

Example:

- The boss suddenly asked me to give a speech at the meeting, so I did it off the top of my head.

218: on a roll

How to use it:

- [someone] is on a roll

Explanation:

- Someone who is on a roll is having repeated success.

Example:

- The new salesman is on a roll. He's sold ten cars this week.

219: on cloud nine

How to use it:

- [someone] is on cloud nine

Explanation:

- Someone who is on cloud nine is feeling very happy.

Example:

- Since she has a new boyfriend, Jenny is on cloud nine.

220: on good terms

How to use it:

- [two people] are on good terms

Explanation:

- When people are on good terms they have a very good relationship.

Example:

- Jack is on very good terms with his neighbors.

221: on hold

How to use it:

- [a plan] is on hold

Explanation:

- When someone's plans are on hold, no further action is being taken.

Example:

- The company's plans to expand the business abroad are on hold until the economy improves.

222: on pins and needles

How to use it:

- [someone] is on pins and needles

Explanation:

- When you are on pins and needles you are very anxious about a situation.

Example:

- I was on pins and needles about my test score.

223: on the ball

- [someone] is on the ball

- Someone who is on the ball is well informed and knowledgeable.

- Seems like the new manager is on the ball. He really understands our business.

224: on the dot

- [something] or [someone] is on the dot

- When an event begins on the dot, it begins precisely at a certain time.

- We will begin class at 9:00am on the dot, so please don't be late.

225: on the fly

How to use it:

- [someone] does something on the fly

Explanation:

- When you do something on the fly, you do it without preparation.

Example:

- I was a little nervous because I had to give a speech on the fly.

226: on the house

How to use it:

- [something] is on the house

Explanation:

- Something that is on the house is free.

Example:

- The waiter brought us some nice dessert on the house.

227: on the level

How to use it:

- [someone] is on the level

Explanation:

- Someone who is on the level is honest and trustworthy.

Example:

- Cathy's new boyfriend is a nice guy and on the level.

228: on the rocks

How to use it:

- [a drink] is on the rocks

Explanation:

- When you have a drink on the rocks, you have it with ice.

Example:

- I like to have my scotch on the rocks, but Jack likes it straight.

229: on the spur of the moment

How to use it:

- [someone] does [something] on the spur of the moment

Explanation:

- When you do something on the spur of the moment, you do it without prior planning.

Example:

- We went to Boston on the spur of the moment and had such a nice time.

230: on the wagon

How to use it:

- [someone] is on the wagon

Explanation:

- Someone who is on the wagon has stopped drinking alcohol.

Example:

- Kim was drinking juice because she is on the wagon.

231: on the warpath

How to use it:

- [someone] is on the warpath

Explanation:

- Someone who is on the warpath is in a very bad mood.

Example:

- Be careful, the boss is on the warpath, so don't ask him for a holiday.

232: on the wrong side of the bed

How to use it:

- [someone] wakes up on the wrong side of the bed

Explanation:

- Someone who woke up on the wrong side of the bed is in a very bad mood.

Example:

- The boss woke up on the wrong side of the bed today, so I would avoid him if I were you.

233: on top of the world

How to use it:

- [someone] is on top of the world

Explanation:

- Someone who is on top of the world is feeling very happy and elated.

Example:

- Tom has a new girlfriend, so he's on top of the world.

234: once in a blue moon

How to use it:

- [something] happens once in a blue moon

Explanation:

- When you do something once in a blue moon you do it occasionally.

Example:

- Once in a blue moon I like going bowling.

235: one off

How to use it:

■ [an event] is a one off

Explanation:

■ Something that is a one off happens only once.

Example:

■ The free coffee promotion was a one off. I wonder what the next promotion will be.

236: open a can of worms

How to use it:

■ [someone] opens a can of worms

Explanation:

■ When you open a can of worms, you do something that resulted in a lot of trouble.

Example:

■ Jack opened up a can of worms when he asked his new girlfriend about her ex-husband.

237: open twenty-four-seven

How to use it:

- [a business] is open twenty-four-seven

Explanation:

- When a business is open twenty-four-seven, it never closes.

Example:

- The convenience store on Main Street is open twenty-four- seven.

238: out like a light

How to use it:

- [someone] is out like a light

Explanation:

- Someone who is out like a light fell asleep

Example:

- I was exhausted last night, so I was out like a light at 9:00pm.

239: out of the blue

How to use it:

■ [something] happens out of the blue

Explanation:

■ When something happens out of the blue, it happens unexpectedly.

Example:

■ My cousin called me out of the blue. It was nice to hear from him.

240: out of the loop

How to use it:

■ [someone] is out of the loop

Explanation:

■ Someone who is out of the loop is the only person in the group who is not informed.

Example:

■ I was out of the loop on project ABC until I got the details at the meeting.

241: out of the question

How to use it:

- [something] is out of the question

Explanation:

- Something that is out of the question can not be done.

Example:

- Jim's wife said that his plan to go to the bar was out of the question.

242: out of this world

How to use it:

- [something] is out of this world

Explanation:

- Something that is out of this world is amazingly good.

Example:

- The steak at this restaurant is out of this world. I recommend it.

243: out to lunch

How to use it:

- [someone] is out to lunch

Explanation:

- Someone who is out to lunch is a bit crazy or strange.

Example:

- The new manager is a bit out to lunch. I don't think he will be working here much longer.

244: over and over

How to use it:

- [someone] does something over and over

Explanation:

- When you tell somebody something over and over you say it repeatedly.

Example:

- I told him over and over to try the pizza in that restaurant. He finally went and enjoyed it.

245: over the top

How to use it:

- [something] or [someone] is over the top

Explanation:

- Someone who reacts excessively to something is over the top.

Example:

- Jack's reaction to the news was over the top.

246: paint the town red

How to use it:

- [someone] paints the town red

Explanation:

- When you paint the town red, you enjoy the nightlife.

Example:

- The girls decided to paint the town red last weekend.

247: party animal

How to use it:

- [someone] is a party animal

Explanation:

- Someone who is a party animal really enjoys going to clubs and bars, drinking and having fun.

Example:

- Jane is a real party animal. She's been out late every night this week!

248: pass the buck

How to use it:

- [someone] passes the buck

Explanation:

- Someone who passes the buck avoids responsibility.

Example:

- The sales rep tried to pass the buck, but the boss knew he made a mistake.

249: pay a pretty penny

How to use it:

- [someone] pays a pretty penny

Explanation:

- When you pay a pretty penny for something you pay a lot of money for it.

Example:

- Len said he paid a pretty penny for his laptop. He should have bought it online.

250: pay through the nose

How to use it:

- [someone] pays through the nose

Explanation:

- When you pay through the nose for something you pay too much for it.

Example:

- Jack said he paid through the nose for his computer repair.

251: penny pincher

How to use it:

- [someone] is a penny pincher

Explanation:

- Someone who is a penny pincher does not like to spend money.

Example:

- Fred is a real penny pincher, so he never treats us for dinner.

252: pick up the tab

How to use it:

- [someone] picks up the tab

Explanation:

- Someone who picks up the tab pays for the meal at a restaurant.

Example:

- David picked up the tab at dinner tonight.

253: pie in the sky

How to use it:

- [an idea] is pie in the sky

Explanation:

- When a person's ideas are a pie in the sky, they are unrealistic.

Example:

- The boss said Tom's idea was innovative, but too pie in the sky.

254: pig out

How to use it:

- [someone] pigs out [on something]

Explanation:

- When you pig out you eat too much.

Example:

- I pigged out on chips last night after work.

255: pitch dark

How to use it:

- [a place] is pitch dark

Explanation:

- When a place is pitch dark, it is completely dark.

Example:

- It was pitch dark when the electricity went out, so I lit a candle.

256: plan B

How to use it:

- [someone] has or [something] is a plan B

Explanation:

- Plan B is an alternative to your main plan.

Example:

- Even if you have a great idea, you need a Plan B in case your original idea fails.

257: play a mean guitar

How to use it:

- [someone] plays a mean [musical instrument]

Explanation:

- Someone who plays a mean [musical instrument] plays that instrument very well.

Example:

- Megumi plays a mean flute and I heard she is good at the piano too.

258: play hardball

How to use it:

- [someone] plays hardball

Explanation:

- Someone who plays hardball is very aggressive.

Example:

- The car salesman was playing hardball, so I got upset and left the store.

259: play hooky

How to use it:

- [someone] plays hooky

Explanation:

- Someone who plays hooky is illegally absent from school.

Example:

- The teacher got angry when she found out the kids were playing hooky.

260: play something by ear

How to use it:

- [someone] plays [something] by ear

Explanation:

- When you play something by ear you improvise.

Example:

- I like to play it by ear when I am on vacation.

261: play with fire

How to use it:

- [someone] plays with fire

Explanation:

- When you play with fire you take a foolish risk.

Example:

- Chris was playing with fire when he had a secret affair with his secretary.

262: pop the question

How to use it:

- [someone] pops the question

Explanation:

- When someone pops the question, they propose marriage to someone.

Example:

- Ben popped the question to Terry last night and she said yes, of course!

263: pressed for time

How to use it:

- [someone] is pressed for time

Explanation:

- When you are pressed for time you are in a hurry.

Example:

- I'm a little pressed for time so I can't eat lunch today.

264: prince charming

How to use it:

- [someone] is [another person's] prince charming

Explanation:

- Someone's prince charming is their ideal romantic partner.

Example:

- Betty said she finally found her prince charming.

265: pull a fast one

How to use it:

- [someone] pulls a fast one

Explanation:

- When someone pulls a fast one, they try to deceive someone.

Example:

- The car salesman tried to pull a fast one on me, but I realized he was lying.

266: put a sock in it

How to use it:

- [someone] puts a sock in it

Explanation:

- When someone tells you to put a sock in it they are telling you to be quiet.

Example:

- After she talked nonstop for 20 minutes, I told her to put a sock in it.

267: put one's foot in one's mouth

How to use it:

- [someone] puts their foot in their mouth

Explanation:

- When you put your foot in your mouth you do something embarrassing.

Example:

- Ted put his foot in his mouth when he joked about the boss in the office without realizing the boss was right behind him.

268: put our heads together

How to use it:

- [two people] put their heads together

Explanation:

- When two people put their heads together they work together to solve a problem.

Example:

- We need to put our heads together and create a new plan.

269: rack one's brain

- [someone] racks their brain

Explanation:

- When you rack your brain you think carefully and for a long time.

Example:

- I racked my brain to find a solution to the marketing problem.

270: rake someone over the coals

How to use it:

- [someone] rakes [another person] over the coals

Explanation:

- When you rake someone over the coals you severely scold them.

Example:

- The boss raked Jack over the coals for being late so often.

271: red tape

How to use it:

- red tape exists [in a business or government]

Explanation:

- The red tape in a situation is bureaucracy.

Example:

- Jim said changing a policy in his company involves a lot of red tape.

272: right up one's alley

How to use it:

- [something] is right up [someone's] alley

Explanation:

- Something right up your alley is exactly what you like.

Example:

- Tom said spending time in a sports bar is right up his alley.

273: rinky-dink

- [something] is rinky-dink

- Something that is rinky-dink is inferior and poorly made.

- My iPod came with a pair of rinky-dink headphones.

274: roll out the red carpet

- [someone] rolls out the red carpet

- When you roll out the red carpet for someone, you give them special treatment.

- They rolled out the red carpet for the new CEO.

275: rolling in it

How to use it:

- [someone] is rolling in it

Explanation:

- Someone who is rolling in it is very rich.

Example:

- Jane bought a very expensive pair of boots. It looks like she's rolling in it.

276: rub someone the wrong way

How to use it:

- [something] rubs [someone] the wrong way

Explanation:

- Someone who rubs you the wrong way irritates you.

Example:

- The new guy in the office rubs me the wrong way. He often makes improper comments about the other employees.

277: run circles around

How to use it:

- [someone] runs circles around another person

Explanation:

- Someone who runs circles around another person is more intelligent than that person.

Example:

- The new boss runs circles around the old boss.

278: run into someone

How to use it:

- [someone] runs into another person

Explanation:

- When you run into someone, you meet them by chance.

Example:

- I ran into an old friend from high school last night.

279: run of the mill

How to use it:

- [something] is run of the mill

Explanation:

- Something that is run of the mill is very ordinary.

Example:

- Jane wore a run of the mill dress to the party.

280: run one's mouth off

How to use it:

- [someone] runs one's mouth off

Explanation:

- Someone who runs his or her mouth off talks too much.

Example:

- Cathy is always running her mouth off on the phone.

281: run out of steam

How to use it:

- [someone] runs out of steam

Explanation:

- When you run out of steam you lose your enthusiasm and energy.

Example:

- Halfway through the race Jack ran out of steam and started walking.

282: run the show

How to use it:

- [someone] runs the show

Explanation:

- Someone who runs the show is in charge of the situation.

Example:

- Tom runs the show in his office and the employees all respect him.

283: safe and sound

How to use it:

- [someone] arrives safe and sound

Explanation:

- When you arrive safe and sound, you arrive safely.

Example:

- Ted said he arrived in Paris safe and sound.

284: scare the pants off someone

How to use it:

- [something] scares the pants off [someone]

Explanation:

- Something that scares the pants of you frightens you very much.

Example:

- That movie scared the pants off me. Next time, let's see a comedy.

285: see eye to eye

How to use it:

- [two people] see eye to eye

Explanation:

- When you see eye to eye with someone you completely agree with them.

Example:

- Tom and his wife always see eye to eye when it comes to raising their children.

286: seen better days

How to use it:

- [something] has seen better days

Explanation:

- Something that has seen better days is worn and in poor condition.

Example:

- Jack's old car has seen better days, so he is going to buy a new one.

287: set in stone

How to use it:

- [something] is set in stone

Explanation:

- When a policy or rule is set in stone it is unchangeable.

Example:

- The company vacation policy is set in stone and it is not flexible at all.

288: set of wheels

How to use it:

- [someone] has a set of wheels

Explanation:

- A set of wheels is a personal vehicle.

Example:

- I think I need a new set of wheels to get to work.

289: set someone back

How to use it:

- [something] sets [someone] back

Explanation:

- When something sets you back it costs money. We usually use this idiom when we talk about an expensive purchase.

Example:

- The new car set Joe back a few thousand dollars.

290: seventh heaven

How to use it:

- [someone] is in seventh heaven

Explanation:

- Someone who is in seventh heaven is extremely elated.

Example:

- Kim is in seventh heaven with her new boyfriend.

291: shake a leg

How to use it:

- [someone] shakes a leg

Explanation:

- When someone tells you to shake a leg, they want you to hurry.

Example:

- We had to hurry to catch the train, so I told Jim to shake a leg.

292: sharp as a tack

How to use it:

- [someone] is as sharp as a tack

Explanation:

- Someone who is as sharp as a tack is very intelligent.

Example:

- The new guy in my office is as sharp as a tack.

293: shoestring budget

How to use it:

- [someone] is on a shoestring budget

Explanation:

- A shoestring budget is a very low and inadequate budget.

Example:

- The boss gave us a shoestring budget to complete the project. I hope we can do it.

294: shoot hoops

How to use it:

- [someone] shoots hoops

Explanation:

- When you shoot hoops you play basketball.

Example:

- My friends invited me to shoot some hoops in the park.

295: shoot oneself in the foot

How to use it:

- [someone] shoots themself in the foot

Explanation:

- When you shoot yourself in the foot, you ruin or lose your opportunity.

Example:

- Jack shot himself in the foot when he insulted the boss in front of the other employees.

296: sick and tired

How to use it:

- [someone] is sick and tired of [something]

Explanation:

- When you are sick and tired of something you are disgusted with it.

Example:

- Joe quit because he was sick and tired of his boss.

297: skate on thin ice

How to use it:

[someone] skates on thin ice

Explanation:

Someone who is skating on thin ice is taking a large risk.

Example:

Tom is skating on thin ice by not completing his report on time.

298: slap on the wrist

How to use it:

[someone] gets or gives another person a slap on the wrist

Explanation:

Someone who receives a slap on the wrist receives a light punishment.

Example:

Ben got a slap on the wrist when he missed the deadline.

299: sleep in

How to use it:

- [someone] sleeps in

Explanation:

- When you sleep in, you decide to sleep longer than usual.

Example:

- It's my day off so I slept in today.

300: sleep like a log

How to use it:

- [someone] sleeps like a log

Explanation:

- When you sleep like a log you sleep soundly.

Example:

- I was really tired, so I slept like a log last night.

301: slim chance

How to use it:

- [something] has a slim chance

Explanation:

- When there is a slim chance, there is a very low possibility.

Example:

- There is a slim chance that it will snow in October.

302: slip of the tongue

How to use it:

- [someone] makes a slip of the tongue

Explanation:

- When you make a slip of the tongue you speak wrongly.

Example:

- Joe made a slip of the tongue when he called his girlfriend by a different name.

303: smart cookie

How to use it:

- [someone] is a smart cookie

Explanation:

- Someone who is a smart cookie is very intelligent.

Example:

- The new manager is a smart cookie. She knows the computer system very well.

304: smoke like a chimney

How to use it:

- [someone] smokes like a chimney

Explanation:

- Someone who smokes like a chimney smokes a large number of cigarettes.

Example:

- Jack smokes like a chimney. I wish he would quit.

305: smooth sailing

How to use it:

- [something] is smooth sailing [for someone]

Explanation:

- When a situation is smooth sailing, it is progressing smoothly.

Example:

- Once we agreed on the terms of the sale, the negotiations were smooth sailing for us.

306: snake in the grass

How to use it:

- [someone] is a snake in the grass

Explanation:

- Someone who is a snake in the grass is an untrustworthy person.

Example:

- Jane said her boyfriend was a snake in the grass and he cheated on her.

307: snow job

How to use it:

- [someone] gives another person a snow job

Explanation:

- When someone gives you a snow job they tell you an obvious lie.

Example:

- The student gave his teacher a snow job about not having the homework.

308: snowed in

How to use it:

- [someone] is snowed in

Explanation:

- When you are snowed in you can't easily move around due to a heavy snow storm.

Example:

- We are snowed in, so let's build a fire in the fireplace and relax.

309: spend money like water

How to use it:

- [someone] spends money like water

Explanation:

- Someone who spends money like water spends a lot of money easily and quickly.

Example:

- Tom spends money like water. He's been to Las Vegas several times this year.

310: spitting image

How to use it:

- [someone] is the spitting image of [another person]

Explanation:

- Someone who is the spitting image of another person looks just like that person.

Example:

- Jack is the spitting image of his father. He's tall, with blonde hair and blue eyes.

311: spread like wildfire

How to use it:

- [something] spreads like wildfire

Explanation:

- News or gossip that spreads like wildfire spreads quickly.

Example:

- The news about the company bonuses spread like wildfire. Everyone was happy.

312: square meal

How to use it:

- [someone] eats a square meal

Explanation:

- A square meal is a healthy and substantial meal.

Example:

- For a healthy life, you should eat 3 square meals daily and avoid smoking.

313: squeaky clean

How to use it:

- [something] is squeaky clean

Explanation:

- Something that is squeaky clean is very clean.

Example:

- I polished the old statue, now it is squeaky clean. It looks new!

314: state of the art

How to use it:

- [something] is state of the art

Explanation:

- Something that is state of the art is the newest and most advanced thing.

Example:

- This new smartphone is state of the art, but a little difficult to use.

315: stay up until all hours of the night

How to use it:

- [someone] stays up until all hours of the night

Explanation:

- When you stay up until all hours of the night, you are awake until a very late time.

Example:

- On the weekend, I stay up until all hours of the night and play video games.

316: steal one's heart

How to use it:

- [someone] steals another person's heart

Explanation:

- When someone steals your heart, you fall in love with them.

Example:

- Frank said Kate stole his heart. He wants to marry her.

317: steamed up

How to use it:

- [someone] is or gets steamed up

Explanation:

- Someone who is steamed up is very upset.

Example:

- Jack was very steamed up when he saw his girlfriend in the cafe with another guy.

318: step on it

How to use it:

- [someone] steps on it

Explanation:

- When you step on it, you accelerate your car.

Example:

- I have to step on it to get to work on time.

319: sticking points

How to use it:

- Sticking points exist in [a situation]

Explanation:

- Sticking points are controversial and yet unresolved issues in a discussion.

Example:

- There are a few sticking points of the contract that we still need to resolve.

320: stone's throw away

How to use it:

- [a place] is a stone's throw away from another place

Explanation:

- Something that is a stone's throw away is very close to you.

Example:

- The café is just a stone's throw away from my house.

321: stuffed to the gills

How to use it:

- [someone] is stuffed to the gills

Explanation:

- When you are stuffed to the gills, you have eaten a lot of food.

Example:

- I was stuffed to the gills after eating the pizza, but it was yummy!

322: sweat bullets

How to use it:

- [someone] sweats bullets

Explanation:

- When you sweat bullets you are very nervous.

Example:

- I was sweating bullets when the police stopped my car.

323: take a dip

How to use it:

■ [someone] takes a dip

Explanation:

■ When you take a dip you go swimming.

Example:

■ It was pretty hot so Joe took a dip in the pool.

324: take a hike

How to use it:

■ [someone] takes a hike

Explanation:

■ When someone tells you to take a hike, they want you to go away.

Example:

■ Jen told her kids to take a hike because she was taking a nap.

325: take after

How to use it:

- [someone] takes after another person

Explanation:

- When you take after someone, you have a similar personality to them.

Example:

- Jack takes after his father. He's good at sports.

326: take one's breath away

How to use it:

- [something] takes a person's breath away

Explanation:

- Something that takes your breath away greatly impresses you.

Example:

- The view at the Grand Canyon took my breath away. I want to go there again.

327: take one's eye off the ball

How to use it:

- [someone] takes their eye off the ball

Explanation:

- Someone who takes their eye off the ball stops concentrating.

Example:

- Jack took his eye off the ball when he was driving and missed his exit.

328: take someone for a ride

How to use it:

- [someone] takes someone for a ride

Explanation:

- When someone takes you for a ride, they deceive you.

Example:

- It seemed the salesman was trying to take me for a ride, so I left the shop.

329: take the floor

How to use it:

- [someone] takes the floor

Explanation:

- Someone who takes the floor begins their speech.

Example:

- The presentation was boring until Bob took the floor. We enjoyed his speech.

330: take the plunge

How to use it:

- [someone] takes the plunge

Explanation:

- When you take the plunge you take a risk and do something new or different.

Example:

- Even though the job market is weak, Jack took the plunge and quit his job.

331: talk of the town

How to use it:

- [something] is the talk of the town

Explanation:

- Something that is the talk of the town is very popular.

Example:

- That new Broadway show is the talk of the town. Have you seen it?

332: talk shop

How to use it:

- [someone] talks shop

Explanation:

- When you talk shop, you talk about business.

Example:

- The two salesmen were talking shop during lunch.

333: tall story

How to use it:

- [someone] tells a tall story

Explanation:

- A tall story is an unbelievable story.

Example:

- Bill's excuse for not doing his homework was a tall story.

334: tear one's hair out

How to use it:

- [someone] tears their hair out

Explanation:

- Someone who tears his or her hair out is very agitated.

Example:

- Jen was tearing her hair out when her date didn't call her.

335: test the waters

- [someone] or a business tests the waters

Explanation:

- When you test the waters, you try something new.

Example:

- The boss wants us to test the waters and open a branch office in Tokyo.

336: the boys in blue

How to use it:

- [police officers] are the boys in blue

Explanation:

- The boys in blue are the police.

Example:

- The tourists were helped out by the boys in blue.

337: the ins and outs

How to use it:

- [someone] knows the ins and outs

Explanation:

- Someone who knows the ins and outs knows the details of something.

Example:

- Jack really knows the ins and outs of baseball.

338: the munchies

How to use it:

- [someone] has or gets the munchies

Explanation:

- When you have the munchies, you are hungry.

Example:

- I get the munchies after a night of drinking.

339: the red carpet treatment

How to use it:

- [someone] gets the red carpet treatment

Explanation:

- Someone who gets red carpet treatment receives a very special welcome.

Example:

- We gave the new boss the red carpet treatment and took him to a nice steak restaurant.

340: thick skinned

How to use it:

- [someone] is thick skinned

Explanation:

- Someone who is thick skinned is unaffected by criticism.

Example:

- Joe is thick skinned so he didn't flinch when the boss was yelling at him.

341: think outside the box

How to use it:

- [someone] thinks outside the box

Explanation:

- When you think outside the box, you think creatively.

Example:

- We need to think outside of the box to find a way to increase sales.

342: three sheets to the wind

How to use it:

- [someone] is three sheets to the wind

Explanation:

- Someone who is three sheets to the wind is drunk.

Example:

- Bob was already three sheets to the wind by the time he arrived at the party.

343: thrilled to death

How to use it:

- [someone] is thrilled to death

Explanation:

- Someone who is thrilled to death is very happy.

Example:

- Jane was thrilled to death when she got the promotion.

344: tickled pink

How to use it:

- [someone] is tickled pink

Explanation:

- Someone who is tickled pink is very pleased.

Example:

- Joe was tickled pink when he got a letter from his old sweetheart.

345: tie the knot

How to use it:

- [two people] tie the knot

Explanation:

- When two people tie the knot they get married.

Example:

- Jane and Chris will tie the knot next month.

346: tighten one's belt

How to use it:

- [someone] tightens their belt

Explanation:

- When you tighten your belt you economize.

Example:

- Jack and Jane had to tighten their belt after he was fired from his job.

347: time and time again

How to use it:

- [someone] tells another person [something] time and time again

Explanation:

- When you say something time and time again, you say it repeatedly.

Example:

- I told her time and time again not to give people food to the dog.

348: too big for one's boots

How to use it:

- [someone] is too big for their boots

Explanation:

- Someone who is too big for his boots is conceited.

Example:

- After his promotion, Jim was too big for his boots.

349: top dog

How to use it:

- [someone] is top dog

Explanation:

- Someone who is top dog is the most important person.

Example:

- Since the manager retired, Bob is top dog in our office.

350: top-notch

How to use it:

- [something] is top-notch

Explanation:

- Something that is top-notch is at a high level of quality.

Example:

- That company provides top-notch customer service.

351: travel light

How to use it:

■ [someone] travels light

Explanation:

■ Someone who travels light has very little luggage.

Example:

■ Tom always travels light because he is an experienced traveler.

352: true blue

How to use it:

■ [someone] or a pet is true blue

Explanation:

■ Someone who is true blue is loyal and dependable.

Example:

■ The sales manager is a true blue employee. He's been with the company for more than thirty years.

353: turn a place upside down

How to use it:

- [someone] turns a place upside down

Explanation:

- When you turn a place upside down, you look everywhere for something.

Example:

- I turned my house upside down for my wallet and finally found it under my bed.

354: under fire

How to use it:

- [someone] or a business is under fire

Explanation:

- A person or a company that is under fire is heavily criticized.

Example:

- The power company was under fire for its slow response after the hurricane.

355: under the weather

How to use it:

- [someone] is under the weather

Explanation:

- Someone who is under the weather is feeling ill.

Example:

- Jack was under the weather so he stayed home from school.

356: under the wire

How to use it:

- [someone] does [something] under the wire

Explanation:

- When you do something under the wire, you do it just in time.

Example:

- Joe submitted his term paper to his teacher just under the wire.

357: until the end of time

How to use it:

- [someone] does [something] until the end of time

Explanation:

- When you do something until the end of time, you do it forever.

Example:

- Jack said he would love Jane until the end of time. How romantic!

358: up in the air

How to use it:

- [a plan] is up in the air

Explanation:

- When your plans are up in the air, they have not been decided yet.

Example:

- My vacation plans are still up in the air. It depends on my work schedule.

359: up the creek

How to use it:

- [someone] is up the creek

Explanation:

- Someone who is up the creek is in trouble.

Example:

- Joe is up the creek because he missed the deadline to submit his report to the teacher.

360: veg out

How to use it:

- [someone] vegges out

Explanation:

- When you veg out you relax doing nothing in particular.

Example:

- I like to spend some time at night just vegging out to relax.

361: walk in the park

How to use it:

- [something] is a walk in the park

Explanation:

- Something that is a walk in the park is very easy.

Example:

- Selling my antique computer was a walk in the park. I had a lot of offers for it.

362: watering hole

How to use it:

- [a bar or pub] is a watering hole

Explanation:

- A watering hole is a bar.

Example:

- After work we went to the local watering hole for cocktails.

363: wet behind the ears

How to use it:

■ [someone] is wet behind the ears

Explanation:

■ Someone who is wet behind the ears is inexperienced.

Example:

■ The new salesman is wet behind the ears. I think he needs a lot of training.

364: work against the clock

How to use it:

■ [someone] works against the clock

Explanation:

■ When you work against the clock, you do something quickly because there is not much time.

Example:

■ We were working against the clock to finish the project and finally got it done.

365: work like a dog

How to use it:

- [someone] works like a dog

Explanation:

- When you work like a dog you work very hard.

Example:

- We worked like a dog to finish the project and it was a big success.

366: worth one's salt

How to use it:

- [something] is worth [someone's] salt

Explanation:

- Someone who is worth their salt deserves respect from others.

Example:

- I think the new boss is someone who is worth his salt. He really knows this business.

367: zip it

How to use it:

- [someone] zips it

Explanation:

- When you tell someone to zip it, you are telling them to stop talking.

Example:

- The kids were noisy, so the teacher told them to zip it.

368: zonk out

How to use it:

- [someone] zonks out

Explanation:

- When you zonk out, you fall asleep quickly.

Example:

- I zonked out on the sofa last night.

Congratulations! You've reached the end of the book and have probably discovered I've actually put 368 Idioms here! I hope you enjoyed my surprise. Thanks again for studying with me ☺

Other books by Michael DiGiacomo:

Like idioms? Get Volume 2 - 365 More Idioms!!

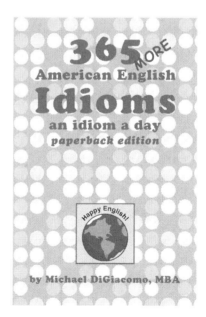

Made in the USA
Columbia, SC
15 November 2024

46616489R00111